NOTE FROM THE PUBLISHER

This journal and the letter accompanying it were found by a wanderer on a bench in a deserted Italian train station in the middle of the night. How it got into the hands of this publisher is an incredible tale in itself, perhaps better left for another time. To the best of our abilities, we have reproduced it as we received it. We assume the author would want it that way.

Perhaps you are wandering as well and maybe it is fitting that you find it now.

February 8th, 1963

Dearest Angelica,

It has been a long time since we've spoken. I'll always remember that day we went our separate ways, each of us searching for our own place in this world. How young we were and how strange it is now to think of the tears.

This package I send you isn't about that, though. I've never forgotten our running joke about the foolishness of mankind. And how we vowed that night lying on the lumpy mattress in your dorm that if either of us ever learned anything truly of value, we would find the other and share what we had learned. Well, here goes. . .

I was sent to an island called Sakahara by my employer, Hanna Food Industries. (Surprised? I went back to college, finally, and became an agricultural genetic engineer.) My assignment was to investigate the island as a possible source of mangoes. If it proved worthwhile, the company was planning to install a cannery there to make use of the abundance of potential cheap labor. And my bosses pointed out that Hanna would bring the impoverished people of this backward island all the good that civilization has to offer.

Apparently, the guy who usually handles Hanna's agricultural fieldwork is highly allergic to mangoes, so by strange coincidence, or fortuitous twist of fate, I was assigned to go. The plan was for me to pose as someone not from the company. They were afraid if the company's interest was known, the people of the island would smell money and get greedy. I was thinking of that pot calling the kettle black, but it was my first decent job after getting my degree and a huge opportunity to make points with the higher-ups. And it sounded kind of exciting.

I was masquerading as an entomologist, a bug collector. I know you must be laughing now reading this, no doubt remembering that spider incident at Lilly's. So laugh! To make it all look real I brought entomology journals and an insect encyclopedia as well as my camera and my agricultural reference books.

The trip was supposed to last a little over a week. The company wanted notes and photos of the various mangoes indigenous to the island, studies on the conditions of the trees, fruit and soil samples, a map of the terrain, and suggestions for potential sites for the cannery. As is often the case, however, the plans we make are rarely what is planned for us. What I learned here was something totally different from what I expected. And you know me and my penchant for keeping journals. (Some things don't change.)

I'm sending you this journal because I'm uncertain as to whether I will return home in the near future — and a promise is a promise. You see, I met a teacher named Katchumo and that is where all of this really begins.

So, there you are. I trust your mother hasn't moved and she'll know where to find you. It's my hope that sending this to you care of her was a wise idea. And if you're reading this, it was. This journal is yours now. May you find in it at least some of the things you've been looking for, and know that I love you.

Love Always,

J.

P.S. — A quick note about the "chapter headings." I slipped them in later, on scraps of paper when I was rereading things; kind of as a game I was playing with myself. But you'll see.

Sunday night 9:52

Am I really here? Umpteen hundreds of miles flown! A five-hour boat trip to an island, an odoriferous mule ride through a jungle to a valley, then by foot half a day, across a river to get to... another mule to a small dock with a boat and some people boarding. My guide for the day, I still can't figure out his name, but it reminded me of Rikki-Tikki-Tavi, then said, "This boat will take you there." I paid my fare (the equivalent of seven cents) to the boat's three-toothed captain and I got on board.

I arrived at Sakahara just before sunset. I waved some money around. An elderly woman with skin the color of earth came to me. Her ample figure was draped in a red-flowered sundress. Her hair was woven with strands of the same bright material. I tried to explain my needs. She didn't speak English but, understanding anyway, she led me to this hut about twenty minutes' walk from the dock.

It's lovely. Tiny, made of bamboo, rope, mud, and palm leaves. It has an intricately woven, very comfortable hammock, a chair, a candle on the dirt floor, and a couple more chairs outside on a covered patio.

Looking out one of the glassless windows, I thought I saw a man in the shadows leaning against a tree. The woman motioned for me to sleep here. I tried to give her my money but she just smiled and left. I looked out the window again. The man was gone. I lit the candle, began writing this, and can hardly believe I'm here.

Monday   10:12 a.m.

   I woke up at dawn and watched the sky change. The birds sing
differently here. It's so beautiful, but I don't know this strange place
and am feeling anxious. Why? Maybe I'm just lonely. It's so quiet.
No TV. No radio. No traffic noises. Peaceful! I'm not used to peaceful.
   I should get to work. First mission — to familiarize myself with
the island's terrain.

Way #1

Eating the Mango
Where the Sky Begins

I was probably twenty steps down the dirt path that leads to my hut when I met him. He was sitting in a lotus position underneath a tree smiling at me coming down the path as if he'd been expecting me.

"There are seventeen ways to eat a mango," he said matter-of-factly.

Needless to say, I was taken aback. How could he be onto me? How could he know and who was he anyway? My heart raced.

"I'm an entomologist," I answered guiltily.

He was a honey-colored old man, small, with close-cropped black and gray hair. I noticed he had a little potbelly.

"Yes. An entomologist," I repeated more to convince myself.

"A big word. It doesn't really matter though, does it? The fact remains. There are seventeen ways to eat a mango."

He was holding a mango in front of himself at eye level, displaying it as if it were the key to the universe. Whether it was the way he looked, the singsong quality of his far-away accent, the way he held the mango, or the mango itself, I was transfixed. I moved closer.

"One way..." He didn't ask my name, who I was, didn't tell me to have a seat, no questions, just simply, "One way can be learned by starting to see the magic in everything. Sometimes it seems to be hiding but it is always there. Look at the flowers of this mango tree."

He pointed up with his other hand but kept his gaze on me. As I looked up I swear it seemed as if the entire mango tree we were under went into full bloom right before my eyes. Universes of tiny white blossoms clustered in dazzling bouquets set off against big bright green leaves everywhere I looked. And from these flowers, the perfume of a sweet and spicy heaven.

"The funny thing is . . . " He paused to kiss the mango reverently. "The more we can see the magic in one thing, a tiny flower, a mango, someone we love, then the more we are able to see the magic in everything and in everyone."

He smiled for a long while. "Practice seeing miracles everywhere. . . Do you see the mango in the flower? Do you see the flower in the mango?" Cutting the mango with his long thumbnail, he offered me some.

"Do you see the whole tree in this piece?" I found myself looking for the whole tree in it. "Eat," he said. "Taste the flower, taste the tree trunk, taste the leaves, taste the roots, taste the earth, taste the sunshine." And as I tasted the taste of my favorite summers, he went on. "As you taste all of these things, ask yourself this: Where does the mango stop and the sky begin?".

Tuesday 11:43

I had to reread yesterday's entry just to make sure I didn't dream it last night. Last night? Has it only been two nights since I arrived here? My time is all messed up. I woke up today and the sun was high. I looked to see what time it was: 11:43. It took me hours to realize my watch had stopped. I shook it. Whacked it on my knee. It will say

11:43 until the end of time or until I get it to a watchmaker. A little

while ago I stopped just short of pounding in its face with a coconut.

A hint of aggression? Well, maybe.

It's this place.

I spent the whole day trying to get a handle on the island, and just

when I thought I knew a path or a beach or a stream, and my way

back to my hut (which, incidentally, nobody has come to collect payment

on yet), I found I was completely lost. On a good note, of course, I

eventually did find my way back to this hut and on the way I tried

more mangoes. They are everywhere and all as incredible as that first one

Katchumo gave me. The fellow I met yesterday — what a name. Sounds like a sneeze. He told it to me just before he said "good-bye" and vanished. I'm sure I must have watched him walk away, but I can't really remember seeing him go.

As for the mangoes — the company is going to flip. I should be happy, right? Then why do I feel such a sense of frustration? Maybe it's just that I haven't eaten well. Besides the mangoes, I dined on one of the cans of tuna fish I packed for an emergency. There are no inns or restaurants. I was not prepared for this.

Anyway, tomorrow I really will collect samples. The sooner I do, the sooner I can get back to the real world — newspapers, Taylor's for steak and potatoes, TV! I just heard rustling outside. I'm looking out my door but see no one. Just a monkey or a hungry jaguar? I'm too sleepy to be scared.

Well, it's getting late — seventeen minutes to midnight (ha!). To bed. Or hammock as the case may be.

Monday, Tuesday, Wednesday, Thursday, Friday, Saturday, Sunday —
Pick any one of the above. I give up on dating this thing.

It's been raining for what I think to be two days. Raindrops the size of coconuts. These raindrops can only be experienced to be believed.

I haven't been able to do any work. Sometime in the late afternoon I broke down. I was tired and hungry and I just wanted to go back home. I began arguing with myself and the walls of this empty hut.

"I am an agricultural genetic engineer. My job is to grow stronger, disease-resistant strains of wheat. My job is to make roses smell sweeter and popcorn pop bigger. In laboratories and greenhouses with neat gravel walkways. I am not a rogue explorer! I need dry clothes, three meals a day, a flushing toilet, nice-smelling shampoo."

That just got me remembering one or two other necessities the island lacked. And, as is my talent, even more than genetic engineering, I spun myself into a truly great depression. I wanted to run, but there was nowhere to go if I didn't want to be drowned by a gigantic raindrop.

A gigantic raindrop? Does that sound as crazy as I think it does?

So, here I am in this muddy hut, in the middle of nowhere, overwhelmed by the whole direction of my life, the loneliness and uncertainty.

Stopped writing for a moment. Katchumo, the old man, came to my door. He offered, "If you would like, tomorrow I can help you find your way around."

I nodded. He bowed and then gracefully wandered off dancing between the raindrops, leaving me confusingly comforted.

I quickly called out to him. "Hey, how do you do that? I get drenched if I just step out for a second. You're dry and all the way

down the path."

    "Perhaps you are trying to dodge the raindrops. Walk through

the space between them."

Journal, please keep me sane! I woke up a few moments ago. I don't

know what trance I was in last night, but I'm back to my senses.

The sun is shining. The ground is too wet for soil samples but I'm going

to grab the first ripe mangoes I see, seal them into vials, snap some photos.

Tomorrow I'll do the soil samples. Then I'm out of here. Done with this island and that crazy old man. I actually dreamt about the space between the raindrops last night — Angelica and I were dancing through it. Funny to be thinking of her again after so long.

Ways Two and Three

The Smiling Way

and

Eating Mango While Singing

It's the evening now. Same day as previous entry. He sidetracked me! We sang! We sang the whole day away. What would Hanna Food Industries say to that?

I was by a gentle stream, not far from my hut, sprinkling mango pieces with sulfur dioxide powder to preserve them before sealing them into vials. In my mind I was already accepting praise (and bonus $$$) for a job well done. Then Katchumo appeared. He crossed his legs and sank down to watch. I was totally flustered. He seemed genuinely curious about what I was doing. I felt bad I had to lie.

"These mangoes are so good I want to save some for my friends back home."

He listened so innocently I felt ashamed.

"You will give your friends these mangoes, yes. But will they know how to eat them properly? Could they answer this question? Do you eat the mango or does the mango eat you?"

"Excuse me," I said.

"Mangoes are people food." He pointed to the sealed vials. "And bird food and animal food and insect food, Bugwon."

"Bugwon?"

"Bug-One. You are one who studies bugs, no, Bug-one?" He went on. "And people, birds, animals, and insects in time become plant food." He reached for a piece of mango I hadn't packed and popped it into his mouth. "So, would these friends of yours know how to eat mango while singing?"

"What does plant food have to do with singing?" I packed

another vial.

"Everything. You see, Bug-One, there is confusion in this world about

the nature of our physical existence and the fact of our inevitable deaths.

The world spins. Souls enter and depart. Overwhelming, mysterious."

He opened his arms and drank in the world. "Ahh, and sometimes one

can become so serious about mysterious." He smiled at his own rhyme then

he put his foot over his head and made a funny face by pushing his

nose in and sticking out his tongue. "Serious is fine but try to smile

when serious. The more serious, the bigger the smile. That reminds me.

Eating mango while smiling is one of my favorite ways."

He popped another piece into his mouth and grinned elfishly while he chewed. "And by the look on your face it's a way you could practice right now. Helps a lot. Even in serious times. This dream is a game, you know."

Then he started to hum. A strange, simple song, the melody sculpted from a scale of notes that seemed to come from lifetimes ago. There by the gentle stream, in the jungle, with beams of light dancing through the trees, he began singing this:

When my body dies and my soul set free,

this tree will make a meal of me.

A perfect circle as any can be

as I eat the mango to feed the tree,

to eat the mango to feed the tree.

I followed him for the rest of the day through the island's streams, waterfalls, beaches, meadows, and jungles. Was that really me? Laughing, dancing, and "eating mango while singing"?

Katchumo fixed bean curd and jasmine rice for dinner. His hut is slightly larger than mine and very basic. The one elaborate thing in it is a miniature orchid plant with one rust-speckled yellow flower. It grows out of a large tin can, artfully fashioned into a metallic sunflower with petals haphazardly swirling everywhere. I looked at that can in the window for a long while trying to figure out what it reminded me of.

I didn't realize how hungry I was until the food touched my lips. It was delicious and satisfying.

"Eat." He gave me a third helping. "You will need strength for tomorrow. Somasha Tahtee. A very important day on this island."

I was too hungry to ask questions. As soon as I was full he walked with me in silence down the short path to my hut. He bowed and disappeared.

Tasting the Mango by Giving It Away

Way number 4

What an incredible day. Where to start? Well, the whole human population of Sakahara, the children, teenagers, adults, and the elderly picked mangoes from trees everywhere. Wherever you looked there were women picking mangoes, carrying them in their turned up sundresses,

Kids climbing trees picking the highest mangoes and dropping them to other kids on the ground. There were old folks carefully plucking ones they could reach. Even infants were crawling to fallen ones in the grass. Lucky I came when I did! How wonderful to be a part of all of this. I was a link in a chain that passed full baskets of mangoes, person by person, down to the harbor to be loaded onto the three boats that would sail them away to people in need.

I should probably back up a bit. The day began with Katchumo shaking my hammock just before the sun rose.

"Wake up, Bug-one. Wake up. A most auspicious day today. We all have jobs to do. Kivo will explain yours as he takes you to your post."

Fiendishly trying to rub the sleep from my eyes I protested,

"I have my own work to do."

Katchumo ignored me and introduced me to a young man in his late teens. He was tall for this island, probably just under six feet. Long, glistening black hair framed his serious face. As my eyes grew more able to focus I saw he had a broad sloping nose and full lips. A face Gauguin would have painted, albeit without the wire-rimmed spectacles covering his wide-spaced umber eyes.

The old man left us. I threw some clothes on and followed Kivo.

"We are part of the basket chain that will carry the fruit to the harbor. Katchumo tells me you are a friend and to treat you as one." (Kivo seemed unsure of the "friend" part. Or was it merely my projection?)

"... Any questions you have, please feel free to ask."

His voice was soft, his English perfect, with no traces of Katchumo's flavorful accent.

As we worked, Kivo explained that this special harvest day comes once a year. The islanders call it Somasha Tahtee. Loosely translated it means "Day To Honor Abundance Everywhere." Not one mango picked on Somasha Tahtee is consumed by the islanders. Every mango is given away. To countries far off, to people they don't know.

I lost myself completely in the work and the abounding joy of the moment. And these people. I saw the smiles on all the faces, everyone working together, for no personal gain, understanding that Nature brings much more than they can ever give away. I passed another full basket down the line.

At sundown, the islanders stood by the harbor to watch the last mango as it was held up for all to see and then loaded onto the last ship. There were cheers, hugs, and laughter. I thanked Kivo and started to walk back to my hut.

On the way, I came upon Katchumo surrounded by a large group of children. He saw me as I stopped to watch.

"Mayshee Tahtee, mayshee tahtee," he kept saying to the little ones as their parents came to get them. When all the children were gone he joined me for the rest of my walk home.

"The old man watches the children. We all pick mangoes for a while. When they get tired, it's time for games." There was a smile in his voice.

"Not that long ago I could run three full baskets down to the harbor, run back to Hali's Peak, take three more down, and never have to stop once to catch my breath."

We crossed a swaying rope footbridge suspended over a deep ravine.

A small white tree monkey with a black masque and a long tail scampered toward us from the other side and leapt into Katchumo's arms. Katchumo swung the creature around to his back.

As we continued walking I asked him what "mayshee tahtee" meant.

"It is a short way of saying 'Thank you for sharing this wonderful day with me, little one.' Ahh, you are smiling. A good day."

"Yes."

I told him that I thought Somasha Tahtee was beautiful. Kivo had explained that no one would eat anything until the coming sunrise as a symbolic act of faith in Sister Earth, for they knew that again tomorrow She would bestow more of Her abundance for all to enjoy and share.

Katchumo turned my face to his. "You look a little wiser now."

"Yeah, and not one bite of mango I might add."

"Really?. . . Perhaps you learned to eat the mango by giving it away."

Funny, until writing this now, I didn't once think how much money

today's harvest was worth. When Hanna Food Industries arrives to bring

"all the good things civilization has to offer" I wonder how Somasha

Tahtee will fare. The bean counters will have coronaries counting up how

much this tradition "costs."

Eating the Royal Mango

or

A Mango Fit for a King

Way Number Five.

I was collecting soil samples this morning, all the while thinking something was wrong. Uneasy thoughts were buzzing around my head like so many flies. And then, out of the blue, I began thinking of the tin can orchid planter in Katchumo's hut.

I had to see it again. On my way to Katchumo's I realized why. The street vendor who made royal crowns. I must have been nine, Zach eleven. We were visiting Nana and Grandpa's apartment by the beach. Zach and I were walking on the boardwalk when we saw that man and his brilliant crowns made of found things like old soda cans, aluminum foil wrappers, dirty confetti, bits of string and buttons. It seemed to me that

almost anything anyone threw away, this man could make into a crown.
I remember Zach and me trying them on, looking at ourselves in an old faded mirror the man held up. Mine was emerald green, made of 7-Up cans and bottle tops and smoothed down pieces of blue and green glass. I loved it.

"It suits you," the man said in a toothless lisp. He held the mirror with his cracked and stained hands. "You know why? Because you are the ruler of your heart."

"C'mon. Let's go." Zach tugged on the beach towel around my neck. "He smells."

"How much, sir?"

"Seventy-five cents."

I was a few cents short but he sold me the crown anyway.

"Everybody ought to have a crown, remind you of your royalty. Wear it proud, son."

I did. All day long, defying people's odd looks about the nature of my kingship.

When we got back to Nana and Grandpa's, Aunt Jane was there with Ian, Simon, and Lily. Simon told me I looked stupid wearing garbage on my head. Then Lily and Ian started playing with my crown, but it was Simon who crushed it with his feet. Dad took me back to find the crownmaker but he was gone.

I was in his hut telling Katchumo this part of my past, something I had forgotten.

"Your little cousins acted the way many people do. They confuse what is of great value with what is garbage. Ahh, well... I have an idea. Follow me."

We traveled down a footpath that ran along a stream. It opened into a gorge with a waterfall at the far end. Katchumo bent over to pick leaves and things off the ground as we walked. I couldn't see what he was doing with them, though. It was a hard climb over mossy fallen tree trunks and stepping-stone-like rocks to the top of the waterfall. He made me sit on the tall rock in the center of where the water divides and falls off. Then he disappeared.

Reappearing from behind a tree with a mango and a crown of bright green leaves and blue flowers he had woven, he stepped into a simple coronation ceremony. A march around the immediate jungle then to the rock where I sat. He crowned me and handed me the mango.

"I, Katchumo of Sakahara, recrown you Ruler and Sovereign of the Kingdom of your heart."

We sat on that rock and ate a meal of mango, dried fish, and nuts. And I must say, we did eat the food very regally. I even sat up a little straighter than usual.

Walking back he told me this: "It's a simple matter of acknowledging your royal lineage. You come from a long line of kings and queens even if they never knew it. As King of your heart, you are King of your world. So when you find peace inside of yourself, you create a whole world at peace."

I woke up this morning just an average Joe, and now I go to bed a king.

Too busy wandering to make a substantial entry.
I have been a coronated King for about three
days now. I wear my new crown well, I think.

I walked this afternoon through a bamboo forest so thick with growth the darkness was like evening. When the wind blew, the bamboo stalks beat against each other, making strange and beautiful rhythms. Hollow woodblock beats echoing and dancing inside one another.

When I came out of the forest again, I was at a lake. The water was a brilliant blue. So much so that coming from the darkness I was momentarily blinded. Slowly my eyes began to make out shapes, then see clearly again. I saw a man sitting on a straw cushion looking out over the water. It wasn't Katchumo. This man was much older and very frail looking with a long white beard and a high brow. I watched him sit there so peacefully. Finally, I went back the way I came.

Later, I told Katchumo about the man.

"Dragonfly Watcher. He has been at that lake for over forty years.

He likes to watch the dragonflies dance over the water. Here in Sakahara dragonfly season is all year long."

I was nervous Katchumo was going to ask me some entomological question and blow my cover. Who knew dragonflies had a season? He went on.

"Once I was sitting with Dragonfly Watcher gazing out over the water when a little girl came to him and asked what he was doing. 'Ahh,' he said, 'I am studying the lost language of dragonflies. At one time we all used to speak it fluently, but that was long ago, before many things happened. Now we've almost all forgotten...'

"The child pondered this for a long while. Then she said, 'Lost language of dragonflies...that's funny...I talk to them all the time and they never once told me that they lost anything.'"

The real world comes crashing in courtesy of Tropical Radio Telegraph Company. The two boys seemed excited to bring Bug-one a message. I read the telegram the taller one handed me.

Hanna Food wants my report and samples. And they're beyond impatient. As I write this I'm remembering something my new boss said to me the day he gave me this assignment:

"If we get this cannery up and running and it's successful, it will be our model for many more to come in that part of the world. And you'll be in from the beginning. Think about that."

Well, Mr. Donahue, I am thinking. I'm thinking it's sadly ironic, the smiles on the two young couriers' faces. They have no idea of what my response could mean to Sakahara. And her people.

Finally I can sit down and write about what's happened these

past two days.

Yesterday, I was sitting on Coronation Rock where the waters divide.

Too ashamed to wear my crown, I held it in my lap. I have deceived

these people. I have deceived Katchumo. Earlier in the day, the soil samples

were finished. I packed new mango vials and took more photographs of

the wildflower meadows where the ostriches graze. Some giddy brown monkeys

had come down from their trees to play with the strange man with

the camera. For a moment I thought they were actually teasing me as

if to say I was a clown for doing what I was doing for the Company.

It was all in my duffel bag, waiting for me in my hut. My work was done.

Katchumo shouted from the waters below. I could barely hear

him over the sound of the falls.

"The King looks weary today." He sat beside me. "No Peace in the

Kingdom? . . . Litata from the harbor tells me you plan to leave tomorrow

morning." I couldn't believe I was nodding my head. "Before you go, if

you'd like, you could show me those bugs and beetles and things you

study and I could give you our island names for them. We have some

lovely little stories that go with them."

"It's not necessary, really. Thanks, though."

"Well, by that logic, Bug-one, what is necessary, really? You must see a

bit of the other side before you go. So beautiful, one should not miss it.

I was just on my way to visit a friend who lives there. Will you come along?"

He ignored my protests. Katchumo is so proud of Sakahara and so pleased to show me its beauty. I felt I had to follow him one last time.

"She is grace incarnate, Ewania. And that is Sakaharian for grace. Her parents chose a fitting name."

We had just walked the length of Crescent Moon Beach. With its fine black sand still on my sneakers we began climbing the daunting rock formations to where Katchumo's friend lived.

"So you could say today you and I are on our way to Grace... Ha, ha!... Even when we are not on our way to Grace we are on our way to grace."

After negotiating a dangerously thin trail cut into the lava rock of three sheer cliffs we arrived at a grassy meadow surrounded by mango tree-covered hills. There, beside a shaded brook, sat an enchanted cottage. I'd heard about cottages like this in fairy tales told to me when I was a child. I was still breathing hard from our journey. Katchumo, not winded at all, said, "What... you think the path to grace is easy?" I managed a laugh.

He picked a purple spiralflower on our way through the meadow and Ewania met us by the brook. Katchumo presented the flower to her and bowed. The old woman bowed back. They both smiled.

"So this is your friend I have heard so much about." She held my hand in both of hers and I felt a rush of what must be the very life force run through my body.

"Katchumo, you will excuse us, won't you?" she asked. "I must show our young friend the trees. Try the new hammock. I just finished weaving. It is downstream a ways in the clearing."

We walked silently through the hills thick with mature mango trees. Hundreds and hundreds of them. But this grove is unlike any I have seen on the island. There are no leaves or spoiled mangoes on the ground, just soft grass. It's obvious how well kept the grove is. A closer look at the trees and I could see that they were all expertly husbanded. The technique I learned in school of grafting hardy root systems to more perfected fruit-bearing strains of a treetop is exquisitely practiced here.

Over the next hill in a small valley against a high cliff I saw a barn and what looked to be a primitive distilling contraption.

"That's my bottling machine. My little business. Mango wine. Shhh." She put her finger to her lips. "Yes, I grow the fruit, ferment, age, bottle, and label my wine here. A few connoisseurs around the world are my clients. I do it all myself. Katchumo helps me when the workload gets very heavy, but usually this old woman before you is enough to run the winery. And, besides, it must be kept a secret. If I had others helping, the whole island would know in a matter of hours."

"No one else knows but Katchumo and you?"

"One other... and now you. That's all."

"How do you keep it secret?"

"As you can see, this is a difficult place to reach. The trail over the cliffs only Katchumo and I know and the cliff behind us is too hard to climb from the other side. We've hidden it well. Those who come by boat just see an old woman living in the meadow, and they are afraid of her. The tale is, I am an ancient witch who eats people unlucky enough to stray into my clutches." Posing as an evil witch she made her hands into pointed claws. "It's all for the best. Why should the people of our island have to know about money and commerce?" I felt a sting in my heart. "When someone is sick and needs medicines we don't have, which is rare, or when some supplies are needed from far away, or the school needs new books, we have the means to purchase them. It is that simple.

"Come plant a seed with me. I have a special spot for your tree."

She led me to a knoll by a freshwater spring close to the great cliff

and handed me a mango seed from the pocket of her sundress. I

noticed the dried hull was carefully hatch-marked to allow the root

and shoot to come out easier.

We dug a small hole with our hands and then she said,

"Before you plant it, hold the seed close to your heart. Feel the shade

this tree will provide one day for somebody leaning against it looking out

at the ocean. Wonder what they might be thinking that moment.

They might wonder who planted this tree and what they were like.

Maybe a ripe mango will fall into their lap and they will eat it,

contemplating the ocean and their life and your life and my life.

Think of all the great spider mothers and aphids and lizards, monkeys and Chititizee birds swinging and singing and making their homes in this tree you plant.

"All mangoes are connected to the seed you hold close to your heart now. All those that came before it are its brothers and sisters and all those that will come after it as well . . . In truth, there is really only One Mango. It has never died since it came to be."

Holding it, I felt special. I was filled with gratitude that I could hold something so magical in my own hands. I felt the shade it would provide, and for a moment I could taste its mangoes and feel the joy it would bring. I was overwhelmed by the thought of all the creatures who would live in it and because of it.

Ewania resumed speaking. "We are all the same life. The ones that come after us to enjoy the tree that is in this seed you hold are here now. As we will be there with them in their here and now. No moment exists without every other moment that came before it and every moment that will come after. The First Day of the Universe is in every seed and in all of our hearts . . . . The secret is to understand that it has never been nor will it ever be any time other than the First Day."

The sun was beginning to touch the water. As the burning orb melted into a cobalt sea, I planted the seed. Then we met Katchumo back at the cottage. He had laid out a little picnic with goat cheeses, crackers, and a bottle of mango wine.

"Now, it is Bug-one who can wait for us," he said. "The hammock you wove is hard to balance in with only one."

Ewania smiled me a good-bye. She took Katchumo's hand. He led her away down the path to the hammock. Just before they were out of my sight, he patted her behind and winked back at me.

Alone with the wine, I drank more than I could handle. A delicate nectar tasting of a remarkable mix of things. Purple gooseberries, marshmallows and fireplaces, crisp winter apples, and boardwalk lemonade. Its ephemeral taste betrayed its strength. I eased into a deep sleep and woke up today — which is actually a day later — the day I was supposed to leave the island!

I'm tired of writing for now.

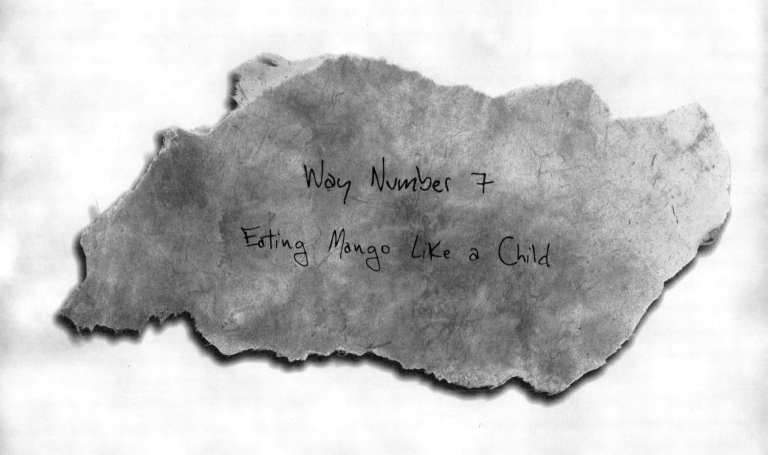

Way Number 7

Eating Mango Like a Child

On our return from Ewania's this morning we were following a path by the Whispering Stream. Katchumo says it whispers many wise things if one listens closely enough. I was rambling on with questions about the various religions of the world. The mango wine I drank yesterday had inspired all sorts of spiritual dreams. I kept wanting explanations for the conflicts that arise from different points of view.

He was saying that the ones who fight each other because of their own beliefs "... are like specks of dirt fighting each other about the nature of their world, refusing to see that they are all in the same mud puddle on the side of the road.

"So many are looking for deep answers to this big question of life. Who am I? Why am I? . . . . Makes my head swim. Perhaps trying to make too much sense of life is like taking a cup of water from this stream because you want to understand the stream. But you soon find that all you really have is a cup of still water, not the stream at all. If you want to know the stream, you must come to her, where she dwells. Here in the ravine, in the pebbles and the moss and the fallen trees.

"Oh, how pleasant for us. You have deep questions and we are so close."

I waited. He reached up, plucked a mango from a branch that seemed to appear only for that purpose. Katchumo gingerly handed me a majestical, ripe fruit with a gemlike luminescence, a pinkish aura. He said;

"Just around two bends is Bisowhe, a small village where a master lives. Bring this to him. He is a little boy called Tali. If you leave now, you will find him playing in the village center. I know his mother and father well, and it will be all right for you to cut this sacred fruit open and offer him one of the pieces without the seed." (Thirding a mango is second nature to me now. Early on Katchumo taught me to slice the fruit lengthwise in three pieces leaving the seed only in the center one.) "When he finishes it, you must offer him the other seedless piece. When both are finished, only then do you give him the seeded piece. Watch very closely every bite he takes. Watch everything he does.

"Bug-one." We locked gazes. "You must understand, it is very important that you observe him with all of your powers of concentration."

He let the silence be and showed none of his usual levity. I felt

this moment was a holy one. Nothing else but fate brought me here.

So many confusing years to what now seemed to be a turning point.

Facing what seemed frightening but inevitable, I felt my body begin

to sweat, despite the coolness of the air. Katchumo continued. "When the

boy has finished, thank him for the lesson, bow to him, and then come

directly back to me."

I found a boy in the center of town swinging on a bamboo

jungle gym. He was alone. I asked, "Tali?" He looked at me, nodding,

so I approached him. I cut the mango with my pocketknife and

nervously offered the first third I was told to give him.

I was expecting a graceful ceremonial example of how to eat the fruit. As I walked to his village, thoughts of this child being an incarnation of a great spiritual master had come to me. What I got instead, however, alarmed me at first. Gently the child took the mango from my hand and that's where the graceful part ended.

He shoved his whole face into it and began chewing. I thought there must be some mistake. This sloppy kid has nothing to show me. I kept watching though, because Katchumo so gravely warned me to use all of my concentration. But the thought of being played a fool wouldn't leave my mind.

He was making sloshing noises as he chewed and breathed at the same time. As he checked the mango peel for fruit he had missed, with juice dripping down his cheeks, he licked around his mouth and began giggling. I handed him the second third. This time was even more messy. It would be fair to say that Tali was totally covered in mango by the time he got hold of the seeded piece and chewed around that.

His high-pitched laughter finally got to me, melted my sacred expectations, and tickled my insides. I began laughing as I watched him finish. I was going to wipe the mango remnants from his face but I changed my mind. He was perfection as he was. I thanked him for the lesson, bowed, and left him smiling with mango juice dripping from his chin.

"Well," Katchumo said, "You were expecting a Japanese tea ceremony from a five-year-old boy?"

I shrugged. He handed me a mango and told me to eat it just the way Tali had. I told him I couldn't. I just couldn't!

"What a pity. Tell me, have you never been five years old?"

So, I took the mango and awkwardly tried to do as I was instructed. And the strangest thing happened. Slowly, very slowly, I began touching that place again. And then suddenly, it was as if some forgotten door in my heart had flung wide open and flooded me with light and fresh air. After a while I found myself sloshing, swallowing, smooshing, dripping, and giggling.

"Let the juice drip, my friend, drip down that beautiful laughing face of yours."

My hand is cramping. I have to take another break for now.

We were still laughing and almost home. Katchumo found a clearing in the jungle for us to enjoy the sunset.

We sat nestled in the roots of a great mango tree and looked over the valley. The sky changed luscious colors as we listened to the music of tree frogs, and the crickets began their nightly concert. There, Katchumo told me that when he was very young he had been a monk of a certain order. I asked him why he no longer was.

"It all began with a mango tree." I looked at him as if to say, You don't expect me to believe that? "Yes, it's true. It seems this life of mine is inextricably connected to the mango." Katchumo ran his hands along the mango roots that cradled us.

"There was a lovely mango tree growing between the homes of two families. It must have been a century old, grand and full with strong branches reaching to the skies.

"Its fruit were some
of the largest and finest
on the island.
The little girl from
one family and the little boy
from the other would climb and
play in the tree for countless hours
a day, and everybody shared its
bountiful harvests.

"Then a tall man came from the outside world, a representative from a fruit and vegetable canning company." I felt my face flush hot and red.

"He found this island with all of its mangoes and saw 'a mine of gold,' I think your phrase goes. He promised untold riches in exchange for the island's mango harvest. As you can imagine, greed can and does visit us all. It came knocking on the doors of the People of Sakahara and suddenly the two families had a dispute about who actually owned the tree.

"A great bamboo fence was built and the tree was in the middle. Whichever fruits grew on each side would be the property of that family. Of course, one family accused the other of trying to pull branches to their side. . .

"Then there was a bigger fight because one of the families claimed more of the tree's roots were on their side so they should receive more of the harvest. The two children were forbidden to play with each other.

"The people of the village finally decided that they could not help the families solve their dispute, so they went to the temple high up on the cliffs at Disradoo. There, they asked the first monk they came upon to come and help. He was young and he followed them."

"You?" I asked. Katchumo grinned as he looked through the years to see himself as the young monk he once was.

"After the monk heard the tale, he asked for an ax. He chopped the tree right down the middle. It split and fell perfectly equally to both sides. But instead of the families looking deeper into their hearts and understanding the lesson they had just received, they became more enraged with each other. Now their tree was dead, and their riches gone, and all because the other side was unreasonable and greedy. And both sides were furious with this idiot of a monk.

"The only ones with tender hearts were the two children. They cried for their tree, and I heard them vow in that moment of sadness to remain friends forever and to love each other no matter what their families thought or did."

He popped into his mouth some of the dried mango and seed mixture Ewania had given us for the journey home and offered me some. The shame came over me again like a tidal wave.

"What happened," I asked, "to the man from the canning company?"

"The young monk and the two children devised a scheme to chase him out. And it worked. But that is another story."

"Is it?" I wondered to myself. Or did I ask it out loud?

Somehow it was night again. Katchumo left me at a fork in the path, saying he had to go elsewhere. I wasn't certain I knew my way home.

"Bug-one." He called out to me and I turned. "You know what to do when you come to a fork in the road?"

"No, Katchumo. What?"

"'When you come to a fork in the road, always take it.'"

Spent this evening looking up dragonflies in Rambur's Nevropteres and the other books and journals I had brought with me. Learned that dragonfly nymphs, tiny wingless cricketlike creatures that exist in the cool of water, live up to a year, some as long as five years. Each sheds its skin many times through the years as it grows until it finally hauls itself up a plant stem, out of the water to shed its last skin, and the fully mature dragonfly emerges. From the time the dragonfly first spreads its wings to dry in the early morning air, most have only two to three weeks to fly away, mate, and lay their eggs before they die.

Weird to think of the elaborate and colorful dragonfly as a geriatric nymph holding on for just two more weeks. Flipping through the pictures of dragonflies in flight I got a notion these lives of ours are as magical and fleeting as the flight patterns of these graceful creatures. Is this really me thinking these thoughts? Good night.

DRAGONFLIES
of Sakahara

a.

b.

c.

d.

e.

odonata Sakarata

#8

No Ordinary Mangoes

or

How to Eat an
Extraordinary Mango

Remembering a lot of stuff from my Past, Journal! When I was a small child I dreamt about being a Painter. I made squiggles and suns and hung them up on our refrigerator door. At about eight I was going to be the conductor of a symphony orchestra. I flailed my arms about to Mom and Dad's recordings of Beethoven and Mahler. Then a couple years later, after wanting to be a tennis pro faded, I was putting together models of the human body. I was going to cure mankind of its diseases. Albert Schweitzer and Louis Pasteur rolled into one.

When is it that a kid realizes he's no Picasso? Or that he isn't exactly a Mozart? I think those are the saddest moments in life. It seems to me that very slowly, unnoticeably, unconsciously, I must have been preparing myself for being ordinary. I learned to "get my head out of the clouds." I started "getting real."

All of that wonder, all of those dreams. How did they become mere childish

visions, things to discard and grow out of?

Just once, I'd like to not make a choice based on "the wisest thing

to do for your future." I know it's a good job and I should be grateful.

I know it's what I've been working for. And I know that if Hanna doesn't

destroy this island someone else will. But are those good enough reasons for me

now? Finally, I am given this chance to matter, even if all I do is just

gain a little more time for these people and their Paradise.

I explained all of this to Katchumo as I reached into the back pocket

of my jeans and unfolded the burden I had been carrying for days.

I handed the telegram to him and waited for him to read it.

TROPICAL RADIO TELEGRAPH COMPANY

RADIOGRAM

Class of Service Desired	
Full Rate	
Deferred Rate	
Message File Number	
Number of Words	
Time Filed	
Via	

	This Line Tolls	Station	Amount
Other This Line Tolls			
Other Line Radio Tolls Land Line & Cable Tolls			
Additional Charges			
Total			

WILLIAM E. BEAKES — *Vice President and General Manager*

Send the following ~~CABLEGRAM~~ ~~RADIOGRAM~~ subject to the terms on back hereof, which are hereby agreed to

SAKAHARA ISLAND
IMMEDIATE DELIVERY

DATED, DECEMBER 07, 1962

To J.

C/O TROPICAL RADIO TELEGRAPH
SAKAHARIAN AFFILIATE 4876-001
QXTY/071262/FRAI2X57BRYT

PROBLEMS? EN ROUTE HOME WITH SAMPLES?
IF NOT, CONTACT IMMEDIATELY.
ROBERT DONAHUE

FULL-RATE RADIOGRAM UNLESS MARKED OTHERWISE

"Bug-one, an entomologist who never once stopped to look at the glorious and rare insects flying about us and hiding in our plants and rich soil? No matter. I will still call you Bug-one. I must show you our haliadise beetle fly. When you see a creature like that, it is hard to doubt Creation's sense of humor."

A few chuckles gently rocked his body.

He handed the piece of paper back to me. My dark secret was out and he treated it like I had just commented on the weather.

And then he was gone.

A few hours later, in my hut, I was coming up with a scheme to thwart Hanna Food's plans. I would contaminate the soil samples with a little ferrous oxide and sulfur, common among the trace minerals and elements that are known to compromise flavor in vegetation. And my "cross section" of mango samples could be from the worst fruit I could find. The only catch is I still haven't tasted one ripe mango here that wasn't wonderful.

I was lost in thought when Katchumo rapped on my windowsill. He was holding a large bowl full of mangoes. "I would like you to find the most ordinary mango in the bowl and bring it to me," he said. "I'll be waiting just over there under my friend the liliba tree."

"Katchumo, can we do this later? I need to find a bad mango. You must have some bad mango trees on this island. And I also need some chemicals. Is there any way to get a chemistry set? Nothing fancy. Just a basic grammar school set. I have to contaminate my soil samples."

Excited to get my plan under way, it took me a while to notice that the old man just kept looking and smiling.

"It's very important, Katchumo. Do you understand? They need my reply soon or they may send someone else looking for me and the island. And we can't be sure that the next person they send will feel as I do."

More looking and smiling as the old man waited for me to finish. His gaze went back to the bowl and then locked on me again.

"Really, Katchumo. We don't have time for games."

"Funny. I thought that's all we do have time for. If I said that to look for the ordinary mango in that bowl is a matter of life or death, would you say no to my request?"

"But it isn't."

"Says you. How about if I told you that world peace depends upon it?"

"Katchumo."

"Would you do it then? And let your scheming wait?"

"Of course, I would, but. . ."

"Then I will be waiting." He sat down under the red-and-orange-leafed tree, and I decided that the sooner I played his little game the sooner he would take me to the bad mangoes I had to send back.

Crouching, I picked through the fruits in the carved wooden bowl.
I figured I'd find a pretty average looking one and be done with it.
But the more I looked for the ordinary one, the more incredible every

mango appeared to be. I was under one of the teacher's spells again

because the skin of each one was softer and cooler than the skin of

the previous one. Each one felt like polished marble, but alive. The colors

became richer and more subtle the deeper I looked. The reds into the pinks,

into the yellows into the greens. Magical swirls of delicious pastels.

And the shapes, individual and infinite. Some as large and oval as ostrich eggs,

some like small pears, some rounder, some flatter. Somehow, each one displayed

a perfect vision of wholeness, each one a version of the Cosmic Egg itself.

I was lying on the floor beside them. I couldn't tear myself away from these glorious strange creations. Each one more mystical than the one before.

In my reverie I heard Katchumo's voice calling. "It's been much of the day. Are you going to pick the mango or not?"

Still entranced I said, "You know there isn't an ordinary one in the whole bunch. You found the most incredible mangoes on the island and put them in this bowl."

"No. They are just the ones I picked today as any other day."

I brushed one against my cheek.

"Bug-one, when a mango appears to be ordinary, it is only because we are not looking well enough to see what is extraordinary about it."

He offered his hand to help me up. "Come, now let us find those

mangoes you need to send back."

We did find them. Katchumo knew of two trees that bore bitter

mangoes. While I preserved and packed them, Katchumo went to town

to request from a larger island the chemicals I needed.

Mango and soil samples, and photos of the most unpleasant rocky

terrain I could find, packed up, shipped off to the company with

a note that said:

"... Prevailing weather conditions made it impossible to

carry on the work. Here it is though, and regrettably

I must say I doubt this package will prove worth

the wait. .." etc., etc. . . . "bad soil, fibrous

mangoes,. . . rampant indigenous plant diseases. .."

Then came my explanation for not returning. In truth, I guess I've

been planning on not returning for days but I didn't make up my

mind until early this morning. I have seen things now in this shining

world of ours that could never allow me to go back to the way I

lived before. I have to move forward but how to explain that to the

company without arousing suspicion?

My note continued,

"... And unfortunately I would also like you to accept my resignation. I am a trained and highly qualified botanical researchist. It was my understanding when I accepted a position with your company that my skills would be put to use in a more challenging way."

Then came the Big White Lie.

"Travel to forsaken islands with diseased vegetation was not in my career plans. If you decide you have use for me in your laboratories, however, please feel free to contact me at any time... " etc., etc.

I knew no self-respecting egomaniacal executive would ever stoop
to ask the writer of such an arrogant letter to come back to work.

I've done it. Feeling more right about things than ever. I think
I'll put on my crown and go to Coronation Rock.

Hello again, Journal. Remember me? Sorry if you've been feeling neglected. Days have gone by. How many, I don't know, but my skin is now a rich chocolate from sitting in the ticklish sun on Coronation Rock, looking into the waterfall, day after day. The spell got broken somehow this afternoon, and I became restless. I couldn't escape the feeling that it was time for me to leave. As beautiful as it is, I do not belong.

I'm not sure where I belong, but my future is not on Sakahara. An unexpected nervousness overcame me. I tried to think it out while walking. I remembered the crown on my head, a joker's crown? I wondered: Have I been behaving foolishly all this time?

I paced through the jungle, underneath chattering trees, worrying, what was I going to do with my life? I have enough savings to last maybe a month in the real world. What had I just done to my career? My future?

And of course, it wasn't long before I came upon Katchumo. He was perched high in the crook of a mango tree, his spine erect against the great trunk, his arms supported by two smaller branches. His eyelids were half open as he spoke.

"Bug-one. How lovely to meet you here. Oh, you have a question. I don't know what it is but I can feel it's another Big One."

"I'm thinking about what I'm going to do when I get back home."

"Have another mango?"

I was about to say, no thanks when he flung it down with his wrist so effortlessly his relaxed demeanor disguised how fast the mango traveled to land splat on my head. Beyond stunned, I froze with confusion as mango

nectar dripped down my face. I wiped it from my slightly stinging
eyes and tried looking up.

"What was that for?"

He was covering his mouth and laughing. He uncovered his mouth
to say, "Well, sometimes the best answer is forgetting the question."

I picked mango chunks from my hair. Then he threw another one,
again splattering on my head. "Wheee!" His laughter sung through the
jungle. Even more dazed this time I began to smile at the absurdity
of this strange situation.

"You see, Bug-one, it's kind of hard to think about something so
big and serious as destiny when flying mangoes are landing on your head."

Another one hit me. And this time I thought to taste it.
Why not? Now I was laughing, too. The mango was delicious.

"Finally!" he shouted, clapping his hands. "I thought I was going to have to throw them all day!" He shimmied down the tree and showed me a brook where we lay in the sun and swam.

Floating on his back, he made ripples in the water with his hands and began speaking. "It seems there is a place on this earth called Anywhere-but-here and many people spend their lives trying to get there. They think their destiny lies anywhere but here. Unfortunately, their destiny isn't anywhere but here."

"So, I shouldn't leave Sakahara?"

He was climbing up another tree now. "This island, that mountain, some city, some desert, Madrid, Sakahara, Tibet. It doesn't really matter." He hurled another mango at my head, too fast for me to dodge. Splat!

"Does it matter, Bug-one? When a flying mango squashes on your head and you remember to taste it, will your destiny not take care of itself?"

I wiped the juice out of my eyes once more and he was gone.

I packed and spent the evening sitting outside my hut watching and listening to the birds and the monkeys, some traveling through the jungle canopy, others preparing their beds in the trees. And savoring the perfume of the nocturnal jungle flowers freshly opening for the night, I watched silvery-winged moths the size of my hands land gracefully on the petals of these giant flowers. In moon shadows, moths so large they seemed imaginary folded their wings back, bowed to succulent sap-drenched stamen, and drank. Just a sip or two, then off to another blossom. I found myself humming one of Katchumo's songs as the moths pollinated the night jungle.

I'll miss it here but I'm ready to leave. And besides, Journal, you're running out of pages.

He came to my hut in the very early hours this morning and rushed me awake. "Come. I have been with Dragonfly Watcher all night. He is ready to die."

I followed Katchumo through dark trails to Dragonfly Watcher's hut. Many People I had seen around the island were there and some I didn't recognize. Children, adults, elderly people. Kivo was there cradling a baby in his arms. They silently welcomed us. The scent was the first thing that hit, cinnamon and cloves. Dragonfly Watcher was speaking softly to each one. One after another, they knelt by his bed and put one ear to his mouth. He whispered a few words, then they would stand up and the next person would kneel and take his hand. As I studied their faces I saw a few tears but no one looked sad. In fact, they all looked serenely joyful.

I remembered when Grandpa Esa died. Everyone in the hospital waiting room, scared and sad, knowing that something terrible was happening. Mom, Dad, Uncle Sol, and Aunt Jane alternated watching us and being with Grandpa. The nurse kept saying there were too many people in his room. Peeking in, Zach and I saw he was all hooked up to tubes and wires. And there was Nana beside him crying.

I watched as Dragonfly Watcher spoke with everyone, then beckoned me. Katchumo motioned for me to do as the others had done. I took Dragonfly Watcher's cool gnarled hand in mine and put an ear close to his lips, not even thinking how I would understand him. It was dreamlike when he whispered one of the only phrases I knew in Sakaharian.

"Mayshee tahtee." Thank you for spending this day with me, little one.

And then I knew to rise and join the others. Katchumo was last. The two old friends spoke no words, just stared into each other's eyes. That was all. Katchumo rose and everyone gathered close around the bed.

Dragonfly Watcher let his head sink into the Pillows
as he gracefully left his body.
Then all around me the islanders'
voices blended in a
glorious song.

Leaving the hut, Katchumo bowed to a shadow at the edge of Dragonfly Watcher's garden. As I looked closer I bowed to Ewania too.

On the way home I explained to Katchumo how I was brought up to see death as a morbid affair. Deathbeds and funerals were bad parts of our lives.

Before we entered the thick bamboo forest, Katchumo turned back to gaze upon the lake and wildflower meadow of which Dragonfly Watcher was so fond. He opened his arms wide and breathed in and exhaled long. As the sun rose it caught tears in Katchumo's eyes. In each tear I saw a rainbow. I told him so.

Lifting a tear and holding it to the sun, he said, "I know. Aren't they lovely."

He took a small mango from his pocket and peeled it. Holding a piece against his cheek, he caught some more tears on it. He handed the piece to me.

"The salt of our tears brings out the sweetness even more."

How to make

Sour

Mango
Chutney

Way #11

Today there will be a feast to celebrate Dragonfly Watcher's life. Katchumo and I made some mango chutney for the event. He came for me in the late morning just after I had finished the previous entry in this journal.

"Bug-one, please try a mango I picked for Dragonfly Watcher's celebration this afternoon. You have become quite an expert on them."

I felt I had been initiated into some special circle. I was proud Katchumo finally acknowledged me as a good student, an authority even, but of course I knew this mango would be as wonderful as all the others he had given me. He handed me the mango with a solemn bow. It felt different in my hand. "But it's hard as a rock," I said. His eyebrows raised as if to say, "You think I don't know that." The mango didn't seem near ripe.

As I cut it I tried to keep an open mind. Even with my sharp pocketknife the mango was difficult to slice. Very unsure, I put a sticky green cube of the fruit into my mouth and tried to chew it. As I spit it out, my mouth in a pucker, Kotchumo laughed and did a little spin. "But, Master . . ." he said, mocking me. "Great Master of Mangoes, if you know so much about the sacred fruit, why is it you don't know an unripened mango when you see one?"

"Okay, I get it. I get it."

"What do you get?"

"Your point. You proved it with the bad mango. That I was proud — that I don't know anything."

"My point? . . . This is a perfectly good mango. All of the ones I chose before I came here are similar in taste. And we will relish them in a few hours."

"But they'll never be ripe in time. These need two weeks, at least."

He was quiet as he perused my hut. Surely, he noticed my things packed and ready for travel. Then he sat on one of the cane chairs under the palm leaf awning. He motioned me to sit next to him.

"Sour Mango Chutney." He smacked his lips. "Delicious. Allow the sourness."

Latchumo got up and handed me the basket of green mangoes. I followed him to his hut. We lit a fire and boiled water. We cut the mangoes into chunks and put them into a huge cast-iron pot. All this in silence.

"Being so sure of what something should be blinds you to what something really is. You were expecting a luscious, sweet, juice-drenched fruit, because Bug-one The Expert knows what a 'good' mango is, right?"

He pointed to my temple and gently tapped it. "If the taste doesn't match what you know to be right and true up here then to you it is 'bad' and you spit it out."

He stirred the mangoes in the pot.

"Sad but true, most people spend their precious lives always between hoping for a 'good mango'. . . and fearing getting a 'bad' one, all the while missing the joy that comes from simply being grateful for any mango at all. Hope, fear, good, bad. Bug-one, if you can calm the oceans of your hopes and fears and the things you think you know so well about the flavor of this Great Unknown Mango. . ."

He paused as he stirred, then handed me the spoon and went to get some spices and bottles from a cabinet around the back. Returning, he continued right where he left off, "...then you can really taste it. 'Oh, it is sour,' you say. Not 'bad mango' or 'good mango' just simply sour mango. Accept calmly and with gratitude what is there. Then gently, gently maybe it will occur to you to add some vinegar, some ginger, some honey, some spices, some heat." He, of course, was doing all of this. "And you make a wonderful chutney."

Katchimo took the wooden spoon from the pot, scooped up some hot chutney, blew on it, and offered me a taste.

"And that is the way to make a delectable sour mango chutney."

He was right, a poem for the tongue — at once sensual, comedic, and comforting. The vinegar announced, the cardamom teased, the cinnamon tickled. The ginger heated my whole mouth so that the honey could soothe it cool again. The journey was incredible, the balance perfect.

I must have had quite a look on my face.

"Bug-one, you would like the recipe." He taught it to me as we poured the potion into clay serving jars.

Katchumo's
Sour Mango Chutney

Cut eleven hard unripened mangoes into bite-size pieces. Place them in a pot and cover with half rice wine vinegar and half cider vinegar. The vinegar should cover the mango chunks just enough to let a few pieces touch the air. (Katchumo says not to forget that the sky is always part of any good recipe.)

Shave one medium-size knob of ginger root (I think judging by the proportions of Katchumo's batch this would mean about three or four ounces) over the mango pieces.

Carefully place six or seven cinnamon sticks into the mango mixture at equal distances from one another. (He told me that there are some on the island who believe that outcomes to questions can be divined by the way the cinnamon sticks arrange themselves when the cooking is complete. His constant joyful tasting as the mixture simmers surely alters the divination results, so he said he's never tried.)

Add six or seven big wooden spoons of honey (Katchumo's wooden spoon looks to be equal to about two of our tablespoons). Mango flower honey is the best choice for this chutney, of course. Wildflower honey also works well.

Scatter a few dried clove buds over the mixture and place the pot on the flames.

Katchumo's fire was gentle. A good simmer is the idea. Leave pot uncovered, stirring occasionally and checking the mangoes for hardness. Once the mangoes have softened, lower the flame and add a few pinches of cardamom, a pinch or two of red

Pepper flakes, a pinch of sea salt, and cook for a few more minutes.

If at any time during the simmering phase the mixture gets too thick, sticky, or dry, add splashes of water ("or mango wine if on hand," says Katchumo) until the consistency is smooth.

Remove from flame. Let cool and serve.

I have to go to the stream to clean up now for the celebration.

Ways #12, #13, #14, #15, #16

4 Gourmet Ways to Eat a Mango
and
One to Drink It

A FEAST!

I could fill a hundred volumes and never come close to describing what I just experienced at the celebration of Dragonfly Watcher's life and Passing. But I want to remember that today.

I tasted the laughter of children,

the dreams of the lonely,

the song of the morning,

the colors of the sunset,

the reasons we're here and the questions we ask.

In between the singing and dancing

WE ATE!

Mango-leaf-wrapped Pompano fish

stuffed with mango slivers

drenched in a mango

barbecue sauce,

mango goat cheese-

coconut soufflé,

Sauteed mango-pineapple fried rice served

in mango-skin boats,

and

Passion fruit and mango ice

with banana sauce.

And Ewania secretly sent some of

her finest mango wine.

Mmmm Mmmm Mm!!!

The Seventeenth Way

I spent the quiet of the morning looking through this journal, enjoying the sun rays dripping from leaves and branches through my window onto these pages. Pools of soft light collected on this dirt floor, these walls, my hands and feet.

I noticed how easily I was breathing, how simple and right a moment can feel. I sat here for a long while. And then as I got up to see if Katchumo was in his hut a funny thought occurred.

Katchumo's first words to me were "There are seventeen ways to eat a mango."

I went back to my journal and started counting all the ways he had taught me. I lost my place a few times and had to start over, enjoying it as a kind of game. I even began to give titles for his ways, and scribbled them on scraps of paper. But even if I included the wine and the four incredible dishes I tasted yesterday, which I finally decided in fairness really should count, I only came to sixteen different ways.

At his hut I found him. "Katchumo, good morning."

"Isn't it, though?"

"I was thinking the funniest thing while counting your ways to eat a mango."

"Numbers for everything, you People. The Number People, I will call you. From now on, introducing you I will say 'and this is my friend from the tribe of The Number People.'" He laughed at his new joke. "Chopping up time as if to chew it easier. Sixty seconds to a minute, sixty minutes to an hour, twenty-four hours. . . . as if Day himself wouldn't know what time Night was coming to The Dance. I wonder, do newborns from the Number Tribe need to know how many sixties and twenty-fours they are before they can reach for their mothers' breasts to feed?

"Yes, I used seventeen to speak your language. But, you speak mine now. And I don't mean Sakaharian."

"Look, it's nothing. I was just enjoying the game of it, wondering if you actually did know everything right from the start. I'm leaving on tomorrow's boat, never having intended to stay this long, and here they are, these ways you taught me, almost to the exact. . . well . . ."

"Number?"

"Yes. Number. It's not an awful word."

"No, but how we use numbers can be." He was not joking. "There are many confused and frightened people in this world who try to turn the magic of our lives into something that can be bought and sold and counted with numbers, using strange notions to decide what is of value and what is worthless.

"But now, let us go on — sixteen, so far."

"So you were counting."

"Bug-one, all humans are from the Tribe of the Number People. I am no exception. I practice seeing through the illusion more than most, that is all. Sixteen, so far, and why?"

Silence. I have learned to wait. Then Katchumo began to sing.

"Your own way,
    your own way,

        eat the mango

            your own way."

It was another of Katchumo's tunes, a melodious greeting from a different world; the notes tumbling into one another like playful children running and jumping down a grassy slope. The strains of his music danced above a mystic rhythm that reminded me of the woodblock beats I heard in the bamboo forest weeks ago. Katchumo danced along with his new song, a sort of free-form jig combined with a shuffle-off-to-Buffalo tap step.

"Night is one end,
   the other is Day.

   In between, the game

   we came to Play.

   Your own way,

      your own way,

         eat the mango your very own way!"

He swung around trees, even got on his back and wiggled his
feet. What his Performance lacked in grace it made up for in exuberance.

"I promised seventeen and there you have them. I think though, seventeen also holds true for ways eighteen, nineteen, twenty, right up to infinity. Ahh, infinity! Difficult thought for the Number Tribe to grasp. It frightens most of us. That is why we had to invent numbers. Hah! Did you ever hear about the man who was looking up at the starry sky one night and realized there was nothing between his nose and the universe?"

"No. I never did."

"Well, the poor fellow was so completely overtaken with fear that he had to go back inside. And he missed the beautiful princess who was out in the garden just waiting to be discovered. . . ."

"Your own way, your own way,

      say what I will I will what I say

          will lead you to find

                your very own way."

He ended the performance with a simple somersault and a resounding cadenza of laughter that set the whole jungle, the entire island, ringing out.

And all of today as I wandered, everywhere I went I heard

and saw the whole world — dragonflies,

rocks, mangoes, trees, huts, people,

roads, ants — singing and

laughing and dancing right

along with the song

Katchumo taught me.

Special Thanks to Nick Bode,
Beth Tondreau, and John Blackford,
the wonderful designers who helped
"find" this journal.

To Will Schwalbe, a Sakaharian
in editor's clothing.

And most of all to my father,
Ellis Kadison, to whom this book is
dedicated. Thanks, Dad, for teaching
me your song. I'll keep on singing it.